MYEOL

To:

Mrs. Ocampo

From:

Giselle

Date:

June 11, 2018

Blessings for a #1 Teacher

© 2012 Christian Art Gifts, RSA
      Christian Art Gifts Inc., IL, USA

Designed by Christian Art Gifts

Images used under license from Shutterstock.com

Printed in China

ISBN 978-1-4321-0151-0

Christian Art Gifts has made every effort to trace the ownership of all quotes and poems in this book. In the event of any question that may arise from the use of any quote or poem, we regret any error made and will be pleased to make the necessary correction in future editions of this book.

17 18 19 20 21 22 23 24 25 26 – 21 20 19 18 17 16 15 14 13 12

Blessings for a #1 Teacher

christian art gifts®

Teacher's Prayer

Lord, please help me
to strengthen their voices,
bodies and minds,
to express their feelings
and control them sometimes.
To explore what's near
and venture afar, but
most important to love who they are.

- Anonymous -

You're a special person!
A teacher who truly cares.
Know that you're appreciated,
and daily in my prayers.

- Karla Dornacher -

He shall give His angels
charge over you, to keep
you in all your ways.

- Ps. 91:11 -

Be of good courage, and He
shall strengthen your heart,
all you who hope in the LORD.

- Ps. 31:24 -

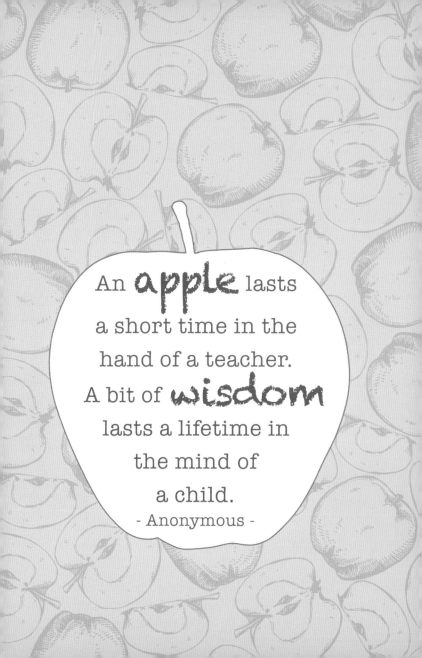

An **apple** lasts a short time in the hand of a teacher. A bit of **wisdom** lasts a lifetime in the mind of a child.

- Anonymous -

Your love has given
me great joy and
encouragement.

- Philem. 7 -

Time spent with children

is never wasted.

- Anonymous -

School is a building that has four walls – with tomorrow inside.

– Lon Watters –

Love is a better teacher than duty.

– Albert Einstein –

Wisdom is more precious than rubies. – Prov. 8:11 –

Love is a great teacher.

– St. Augustine –

In matters of style, swim with the current. In matters of principle, stand like a rock.

– Thomas Jefferson –

You make a difference!

**Commit to the LORD
whatever you do,
and your plans will succeed.**

- Prov. 16:3 -

**Every child is a
bundle of potential
and promise.**

- Anonymous -

Do all the good you can,

by all the means you can,

in all the ways you can,

in all the places you can,

to all the people you can,

as long as you ever can.

- John Wesley -

All our children deserve teachers

who believe they can learn and who

will not be satisfied until they do.

- Joe Nathan -

To **teach**, to **guide**, to **explain**,

to **help**, to **nurture** – these are

life's noblest attainments.

- Frank Tyger -

You are God's workmanship,
created in Christ Jesus
to do good work, which
God has prepared in
advance for you to do!

– Eph. 2:10 –

Kites rise highest
against the wind,
not with it.

– Winston Churchill –

Teachers believe they have a gift
for giving: it drives them with
the same irrepressible drive that
drives others to create a work of
art or a market or a building.

- A. Bartlett Giamatti -

GOOD

Train up a child in the way
he should go, and when he is old
he will not turn from it.

- Prov. 22:6 -

I will instruct you and teach
you in the way you should go;
I will counsel you with
My loving eye on you.

- Ps. 32:8 -

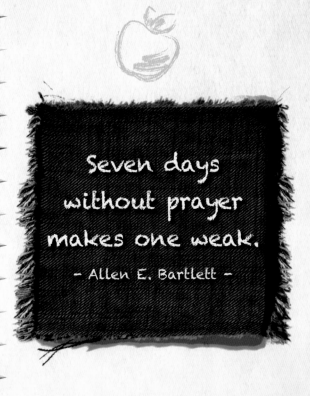

Seven days
without prayer
makes one weak.

– Allen E. Bartlett –

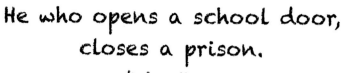

He who opens a school door,
closes a prison.

– Victor Hugo –

An Apple a Day
A Recipe for an excellent teacher:

A is for aptitude – intelligence
to teach

P is for patience – when they're
hard to reach

P is for prayer – when my day's
work is done

L is for love – may I love *everyone*

E is for empathy – a feeling heart.

Mix them together –
and now we can start.

- Melody Carlson -

Children are
messengers we
send to a time
we will not see.

- Anonymous -

I have not stopped
giving thanks for you,
remembering
you in my prayers.

- Eph. 1:16 -

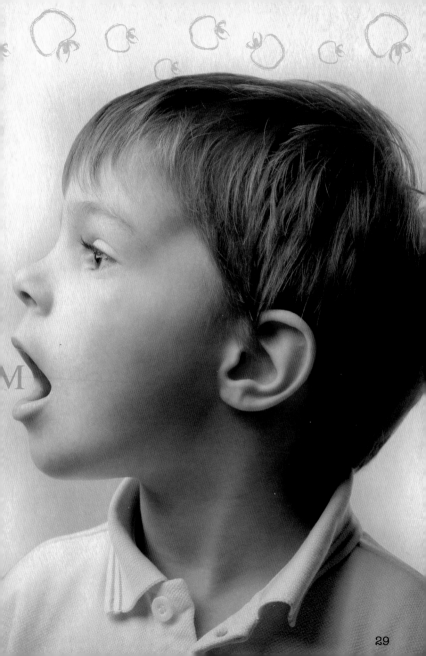

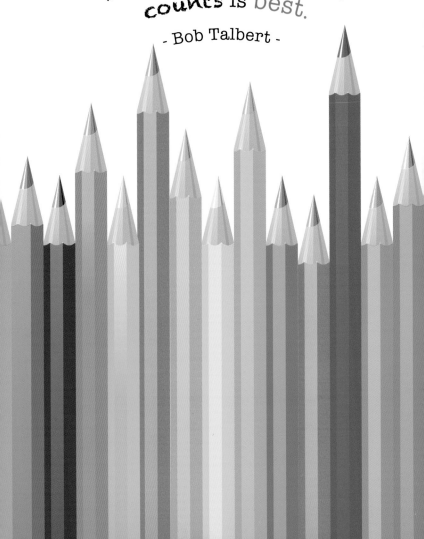

Teaching kids **to count** is fine, but teaching them **what counts** is best.

- Bob Talbert -

Shine as lights among
the people of this world,
as you hold firmly to the
message that gives life.

- Phil. 2:15-16 -

To teach is to learn twice.

- Joseph Joubert -

A teacher affects eternity;
he can never tell where
his influence stops.

- Henry Adams -

Whatever your hand
finds to do, do it
with all your might.

- Eccles. 9:10 -

A good teacher remembers
what it was like to be taught
by their favorite teacher.

- Robert McLain -

Whatever you do, work at it with
all your heart, as working for
the Lord, not for human masters.

- Col. 3:23 -

Wisdom will enter your
heart, and knowledge will
be pleasant to your soul.

- Prov. 2:10 -

a b c d e f
g h i j k l
m n o p q
r s t u v
w x y z

Blessed is the hand that prepares a **pleasure** for a **child**, for there is no saying when and where it may **bloom** forth.

- Douglas William Jerrold -

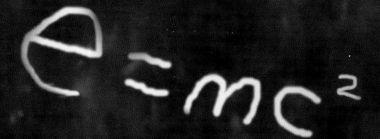

Be **faithful** in **small** things because
it is **in them** that your **strength** lies.

- Mother Teresa -

God regards with
how much love a
person performs
a work, rather than
how much he does.

- Thomas à Kempis -

Do not be conformed to this world, but
be transformed by the renewing of your
mind, that you may prove what is that good
and acceptable and perfect will of God.

- Rom. 12:2 -

In my lifetime I
hope to develop ...
Arms that are strong,
Hands that are gentle,
Ears that will listen,
Eyes that are kind,
A mind full of wisdom,
A heart that understands,
A tongue that will
speak softly.

- Anonymous -

The art of teaching is the art of assisting discovery.
- Mark van Doren -

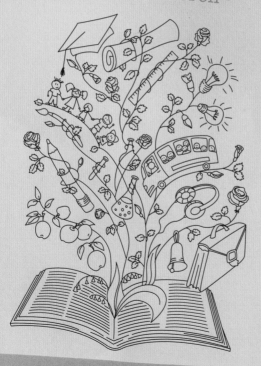

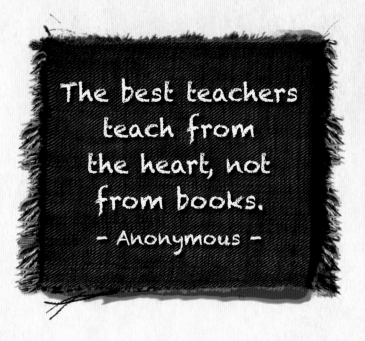

The best teachers
teach from
the heart, not
from books.

- Anonymous -

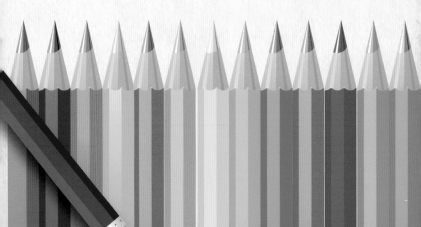

If I can put one touch of rosy
sunset into the life of any man
or woman, I shall feel that I
have worked with God.

– John MacDonald –

Every time I think of you,
I thank God for your life.

- 1 Cor. 1:4 -

People don't care how
much you know until they
know how much you care.

- Anonymous -

Kind words can be
short and easy to speak,
but their echoes
are truly endless.

- Mother Teresa -

Great works
are performed
not by **strength**,
but by **perseverance.**

- Samuel Johnson -